Bridges Coaching

Coaching Culture Certification Course

A publication of Bridges Coaching by Cindy Scott
with Anchored for CARE and thoughts about Nehemiah in the ROAD by Eric Scott.
www.bridgescoaching.net

Editing: Meredith Scott & Uriah Renzetti
Copy Design: Chelsea Phillips
Cover design: Andrew Danglis and Chelsea Phillips
Cover picture: Unsplash

COACHING CULTURE

"Making disciples not dependents."

– CINDY SCOTT
Bridges Coaching

BRIDGES COACHING

Bridges Life Coach Certification Intro

Things you should have:
    Leadership Coaching – text by Tony Stolzfus
    Coaching Culture Certification Workbook -
    teaching notes and course work by Cindy Scott

Introduction Checklist
    Plan to attend group welcome class
    Connect with facilitator to schedule peer partner sessions.
    Connect with your cohort in Bridges Coaching Facebook group
    Start shared google coursework checklist
    (All online connections will be explained in the group welcome class.)

Please note coursework types:

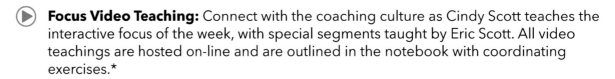 **Focus Video Teaching:** Connect with the coaching culture as Cindy Scott teaches the interactive focus of the week, with special segments taught by Eric Scott. All video teachings are hosted on-line and are outlined in the notebook with coordinating exercises.*

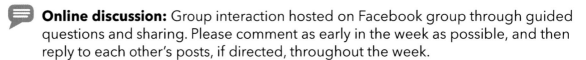 **Online discussion:** Group interaction hosted on Facebook group through guided questions and sharing. Please comment as early in the week as possible, and then reply to each other's posts, if directed, throughout the week.

 **Reading:** Focused reading for each week's topic in our text *Leadership Coaching* may include required exercises. Highlight anything you want to talk about in your next peer session. Also, write any questions in the margins for review in the next week's meeting.

 **Project:** Multiple ways to apply and practice each week's focus.

Peer Prep: Thoughts to prepare for sharing in peer meeting.

 **Peer Meeting:** Facilitated peer meeting to host discussion on material and its application, personal coaching and coaching practicum.
- Personal Coaching: Experience being coached by facilitator and observe your peer being coached. Weeks 2, 4, 6 & 8.
- Coaching Practicum: Experience coaching in and observed environment as you coach a volunteer client. Weeks 7, 9 & 11.
- Coaching Evaluation: Evaluate your coaching in a directed process.

Journal Time: Personal reflection through guided application.

Talk Time: Process thoughts with your peer partner. Share thoughts in facebook message if you aren't able to watch videos together.

 **Group Class:** Meet with entire cohort and facilitators at start, mid-point and final celebration. All course work should be done in order of listing on each week.

* These videos are protected by copyright, for personal use. Any public distribution or sharing is prohibited.

- Focus Video
- Online Discussion
- Reading
- Peer Prep
- Peer Meeting
- Project

▶ WEEK 1 | FOCUS VIDEO

Watch the "What is Coaching?" videos. Follow along with teaching notes, journaling and projects. Share thoughts on Talk Time with Peer if you don't watch the video togeter.

💬 WEEK 1 | ONLINE DISCUSSION

Choose one area of the Always circle and write a bit about how a clear revelation of it can be used in dealing with life and growth. In the "search this group" area on the facebook group page, type "Week 1" each time you're looking for the respective online discussion. Then click the magnifying glass to search.

Reply to at least two other posts started by someone else.

WEEK 1 | READING: INTRODUCTION, CHAPTERS 1 & 2

Do Exercise 2.2 this week.

WEEK 1 | PEER PREP

Be prepared for your Peer Partner Meeting. Be ready to take turns sharing.
- If you are new to each other, share a bit of the basics about yourself:
  - What do you do?
  - Where do you live?
  - Who is in your family?
  - How did you come to love God?

- Also be prepared to share some hopes, dreams, and concerns for this course:
  - Who do you hope to help by taking this course?
  - What do you hope to do with what you have learned? (ex. Enhance your current position/life, become a facilitator or coach, work for an organization)
  - What concerns do you have about this experience?

 ## WEEK 1 | PEER MEETING
Week 1 Review
- Peer Prep questions
- Coaching Reflection- what has you thinking about the coaching paradigm?
- Check in with online discussion, reading, and projects.
  - Talk about Exercise 2.2.
  - How are things going with the Facebook group?
  - What did you like about the videos?
  - What do you think of the text so far? What did you note or highlight?
  - Do you have any questions?
  - Prepare for Wheel of Life Project.
- Explore Coaching Rotation

 ## WEEK 1 | PROJECT: WHEEL OF LIFE
The "Wheel of Life" can be found on p. 297 in the text *Leadership Coaching*.

First, make a copy of the chart in case you ever want to use it again. (Or feel free to just draw on the chart on another sheet if you would like.) Do the exercise explained and rank and shade each area of your life.

See the Master Class at the end of Chapter 9, page 120, in the text for more in-depth explanation of how best to do this project.

Choosing Coaching Focus

Pick one of your lowest areas and prepare to explain what you would like to focus on in your personal coaching session and what it would take to feel like you had a "win" in that area.

Write your chosen focus area here:

_____

_____

_____

_____

WHAT IS COACHING?

What is the first thing that comes to mind when you hear the word "coaching"?

_____

_____

_____

> **Coaching is a set of conversational tools used by trained individuals to come alongside people as a thinking partner.**

Historically, the use of the word "coach" is derived from a vehicle, like the pumpkin in Cinderella or a stagecoach in the Wild West. Coaching is used as **a vehicle to get from one place to another.**

Coaching is helping others engage with God's plan for them!

Coaches help people hear from God and move forward in areas that _they sense God is guiding them_.

Coaching is essentially building bridges. A bridge takes someone from where they are to a place they could not easily get to without the bridge. Coaching, similarly, maneuvers people from one place to another. It takes people from where they are to a place they could not easily get to without coaching.

_____

_____

_____

What is the difference between coaching and counseling?

Lifeforming Leadership Coaching explains the difference between coaching and counseling the following way:

COACHING		COUNSELING
Healthy People	< USED FOR >	Hurting People
Growth	< FOCUSES ON >	Healing
The Future	< LOOKS TO >	The Past
Collaborative	< APPROACH IS >	Prescriptive
Fulfillment	< WORKS TOWARD >	Functionality
Client's Discernment	< DIRECTED BY >	Counselor's Diagnosis

Coaching is the ultimate pathway for mature people to move forward. The continuum below demonstrates a progression that leads to this mature growth pattern.

TELLING > TEACHING > TRAINING > TRUSTING

_____

_____

_____

Freeze-Framing
Freeing people from a frozen place breathes life into who they could BECOME.

_____

_____

_____

_____

_____

_____

> Freeing people from a frozen place allows us to breathe life into who they could become.

✐ Journal Time

Do an exercise like the small group leaders and think of 3 people you work with.
Write their name (then how you might freeze-frame them) and then what they could become.

1) _____

_____

2) _____

_____

3) _____

_____

What could someone freeze-frame you as?

_____

_____

_____

_____

What could freeze-framing keep you from becoming?

_____

_____

_____

Name three people you would like to speak life into.

_____

_____

_____

Wrapping Up

Other paradigms of growth:

Counseling addresses past hurts and feelings.
Teaching imparts acquired knowledge to a student.
Mentoring offers life lessons learned through experience to the mentee.
Coaching assists an individual in connecting with what God has for them.

> **Mentoring is imparting to you what God has given me; coaching is drawing out of you what God has put in you.**
>
> **DALE STOLL**

_____

_____

_____

_____

_____

_____

_____

_____

_____

How Is Coaching Different?

_____

_____

_____

_____

_____

_____

_____

_____

_____

The truth is that God wants to engage with each of us individually. He has designed a plan for whatever unique situation we are facing.

God has designed a plan for whatever unique situation we are facing.

_____

_____

_____

_____

_____

_____

One-Minute Takeaway
Take one minute to write down what stood out to you in this session.

_____

_____

_____

_____

_____

THE **ALWAYS CIRCLE**

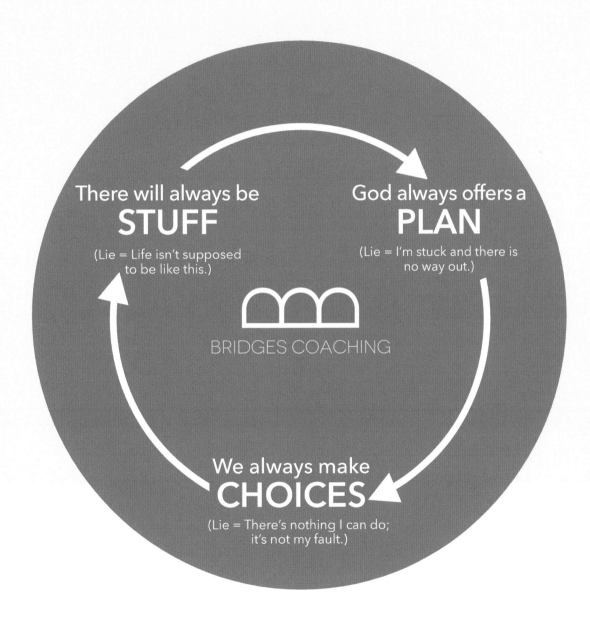

There will always be
STUFF

(Lie = Life isn't supposed
to be like this.)

God always offers a
PLAN

(Lie = I'm stuck and there is
no way out.)

BRIDGES COACHING

We always make
CHOICES

(Lie = There's nothing I can do;
it's not my fault.)

THERE'S ALWAYS GOING TO BE STUFF!

_____

_____

_____

_____

_____

_____

GOD ALWAYS OFFERS A PLAN!

_____

_____

_____

_____

_____

_____

_____

WE ALWAYS MAKE CHOICES!

_____

_____

_____

_____

_____

_____

_____

The Life Spiral

> **With God, life has the potential of always being an adventure.**

✏️ Journal Time

_____
_____
_____
_____
_____
_____
_____
_____
_____
_____

WHAT IS COACHING? TOP TEN

#10 COACHING IS _____

#9 COACHING IS _____

#8 COACHING IS _____

#7 COACHING IS _____

#6 COACHING IS _____

#5 COACHING IS _____

#4 COACHING IS _____

#3 COACHING IS _____

#2 COACHING IS _____

#1 COACHING IS _____

Talk Time
Get with a partner or two and look over the Coaching Top Ten. Share with each other which one intrigues you the most and explain why.

One-Minute Takeaway
Take one minute to write down what stood out to you in this session.

_____
_____
_____
_____

- ☐ **Focus Video**
- ☐ **Reading**
- ☐ **Online Discussion**
- ☐ **Project**
- ☐ **Peer Prep**
- ☐ **Peer Sharing**
- ☐ **Peer Meeting**

Additional Resource:
Christ Centered Coaching
by Jane Creswell

▶ WEEK 2 | FOCUS VIDEO

Watch the "Why Coaching?" video.

📚 WEEK 2 | READING: CHAPTERS 3 & 4

Choose one of the "Top 5 reasons" to be coached that intrigues you most. Be prepared to share in peer session.

💬 WEEK 2 | ONLINE DISCUSSION: BIBLICAL PROJECT

Take a look at the last part of Chapter 4 "Imitating the way God deals with us." Find at least two new biblical examples of the coaching paradigm and choose which of the 7 categories listed suits the verse you found. Comment and add them under the value list in the online discussion.

⚙️ WEEK 2 | PROJECT: COACHING VS. TELLING COMPARISON

Consider the difference between coaching and telling. List at least two pros and cons of coaching.

Coaching Pros:
- _____
- _____

Coaching Cons
- _____
- _____

Telling Pros
- _____
- _____

Telling Cons
- _____
- _____

WEEK 2 | PEER PREP

Take some time and choose a significant spiritual development time in your life when you took a lap around the Always Circle.
- What was the "stuff" that caused it?
- What was God's plan?
- What choices did you need to make?
- What did you learn and how did you put what you learned into practice?

Share your thoughts in a Facebook message with your peer and include your coach training facilitator.

 WEEK 2 | PEER MEETING
Week 2 Review
- Recap the Biblical Project
- How could sharing your spiritual development story build faith?
- Which of the "Top 5 reasons to be coach and be coached" stands out to you and why?

PERSONAL COACHING SESSION
This week will be your first personal coaching session. Come with the focus you chose from the Wheel of Life project last week.

IT'S BIBLICAL

_____

_____

_____

_____

IT'S EFFECTIVE

_____

_____

_____

_____

> God chose to give free will; we must reflect the same.

Biblical Basis for Coaching

GENESIS 3:9 | THE GARDEN OF EDEN

_____

_____

_____

_____

JOB 38:1-7 | JOB AND THE UNDOING

_____

_____

_____

_____

NOW IT'S YOUR TURN...

Work as assigned on the following scriptures, and answer the associated questions. See next page to write your groups' thoughts.

Joshua – Jericho and Ai

- What if Joshua wrote a book after Jericho, what would it be called? Maybe *How to Take a City in Just Seven Days!* but what's the problem there?
- How did the conquest go in Ai (the second city)? Would marching have worked there?
- How did the takeover go after that?
- Why didn't God just give the Israelites a formulaic pattern to follow?

Luke 2:46

After three days, they found Jesus sitting in the Temple with the teachers, listening to them and asking them questions.

- In other gospels it says Jesus was found teaching in the temple, but what does Luke say?
- What do you think He was doing by asking them questions? Did He need the knowledge they had?
- Why was He listening to them?

Mark 8:27-29

While they were traveling, Jesus asked them, 'Who do people say I am?' They answered, 'Some say you are John the Baptist. Others say you are Elijah, and others say you are one of the prophets.' Then Jesus asked, 'But who do you say I am?' Peter answered, 'You are the Christ.' Jesus warned his followers not to tell anyone who he was.

- What was Jesus' purpose in asking the first question first? (Was He unsure of Himself? Maybe He was having a bad day? Was He insecure? Did He need affirmation? Was He creating options for the disciples to choose from?)
- Why did Jesus ask the second question?
- Why didn't He tell everyone clearly who He was?

Galatians 3:11, 5:25

Now it is clear that no one can be made right with God by the law, because the Scriptures says, 'Those who are right with God will live by faith.' (3:11)

We get our new life from the Spirit, so we should follow the Spirit. (5:25)

- If living by faith is different from person to person, what does it mean to live by faith?
- How can we help each other "live by the Spirit"?
- Why doesn't Scripture make "living by faith" more clear?
- How can we know if we are doing it right?

I Corinthians 8 | The "Meat Sacrificed to Idols" Saga

- How do we know if we should "eat meat sacrificed to idols"?
- What are some things in contemporary culture that some Christians do with a clear conscience and others cannot?
- Are there clear lines of what we should do as Christians and things we should not do? If so, how would we know for sure which category our questions fall into.

Group Work

Group Scripture: _____

Group Thoughts: _____

_____

_____

_____

_____

_____

_____

Group Share

Each group will share their thoughts on their verses and questions.

_____

_____

_____

_____

_____

_____

_____

_____

_____

_____

_____

_____

Anchored for CARE

> **Our "anchored place" in God determines the influence of our care for people.**

Hebrews 6:19

We have this hope as an anchor for the soul, sure and strong. It enters behind the curtain in the Most Holy Place in heaven.

Galatians 6:1-5 (NIV)

Brothers and sisters, if someone is caught in a sin, you who live by the Spirit should restore that person gently. But watch yourselves, or you also may be tempted. **Carry each other's burdens,** *and in this way you will fulfill the law of Christ. If anyone thinks they are something when they are not, they deceive themselves. Each one should test their own actions. Then they can take pride in themselves alone, without comparing themselves to someone else, for each one should* **carry their own load.**

_____

_____

_____

_____

_____

COMPASSION

_____

_____

ACTION

_____

_____

RESPONSIBILITY

_____

_____

EXIT/ **E**NTER

_____

_____

Two Word Pictures

SHOELACES

_____

_____

_____

PERSONAL TRAINER

_____

_____

_____

✏ Journal Time

Think of a couple care situations in your life. Write a little bit about what kind of burdens are involved—crushing burdens that need assistance or "rucksack" that need to be carried on their own.

_____

_____

_____

_____

_____

_____

_____

_____

_____

_____

_____

This time we talked about how coaching is Biblical and looked at several Biblical examples, as well as a more in-depth look at the two kinds of burdens in Galatians 6. We also looked at a couple great word pictures that connect with coaching.

Take a moment and review this lesson. Pick one of the sentences below, write out your ending, and be prepared to share it with the group.

The Biblical example that has me thinking the most is _____
because _____
_____

Understanding that there are two kinds of "burdens" changes everything,
because _____
_____

The Word picture that has me thinking is _____
because _____
_____

⧗ One-Minute Takeaway
Take one minute to write down what stood out to you in this session.

_____
_____
_____
_____
_____
_____

BRIDGES COACHING

Coaching Session   Date: _____

Focus:_____

_____

_____

Coaching Appointment Notes:_____

_____

_____

_____

_____

_____

_____

_____

Action Steps for Next Coaching Appointment:

☐ _____

☐ _____

☐ _____

☐ _____

☐ _____

Concerns or Challenges:_____

_____

_____

_____

_____

_____

_____

NEXT APPOINTMENT   Date: _____   Time: _____

BRIDGES COACHING

Coach Form

Client Name: _____   Date: _____

Client Progress Report:_____

_____

_____

_____

_____

_____

_____

_____

Focus:_____

_____

_____

Coaching Appointment Notes: _____

_____

_____

_____

_____

_____

_____

Action Steps for Next Coaching Appointment:_____

_____

_____

_____

_____

_____

NEXT APPOINTMENT   Date: _____   Time: _____

BRIDGES COACHING

COACHING EVALUATION

Assess the coaching session you observed.

Coaching Asssessment

What percentage of the time was the coachee talking? _____

What was the goal of the client? _____
_____
_____

What was the most powerful question? _____
_____

What would you say was the strong suit in this session? _____
_____
_____

What action step(s) were agreed upon?
_____
_____
_____
_____
_____
_____
_____

Any questions you have:
_____
_____
_____
_____
_____

WEEK 3 COURSEWORK: JOURNEYING

- Focus Video
- Reading
- Online Discussion
- Project
- Peer Prep
- Peer Meeting

▶ WEEK 3 | FOCUS VIDEO

Watch the "Journeying" videos.

📚 WEEK 3 | READING: CHAPTERS 5 & 6

Pick one of the coaching values in Chapter 6 that you want to lean into more, and be prepared to discuss it in your peer meeting.

Pick at least one thing you would like to share from the reading. It could be something you liked, something you wanted to talk more about or even something you didn't understand or agree with.

💬 WEEK 3 | ONLINE DISCUSSION: WHY IS IT SO HARD TO TRUST?

Write a post about why it is hard to trust that God has a plan when we are in the midst of stuff.

Comment on at least one other post.

⚙ WEEK 3 | PROJECT: METACOGNITION AWARENESS

Metacognition means thinking about what you are thinking about. It's a fancy way of saying that there is a conversation happening inside your head while you are having conversations with other people.

During your conversations this week, become aware of what is going in your head while you are having conversations with others. Consider at least three conversations with different people. Write their name and the conversation topic under the possible thoughts listed below.

If you have a recurring thought that is not listed feel free to add it at the end where the blanks are located. Be prepared to discuss in your next peer partner meeting.

• I went through the same thing, only worse. Shall I tell them?

_____

• I don't know what they want me to do about this. It's their problem, but I am the one feeling stuck.

_____

• God, where are You? How can this be happening?

_____

• I know exactly what they should do. If they would only listen to me, I could fix this.

_____

• I don't know if I can listen to this same thing one more time.

_____

• I can't believe they can't see what's wrong. It's so clear.

_____

• How can anyone be expected to get through this? It's too much to bear.

_____

• I'm overwhelmed. I have no idea how to respond.

_____

• Other: _____

WEEK 3 | PEER PREP

Think about a time when someone was vulnerable with you and trusted you by sharing something personal. Be prepared to share the story.

Think about a time when you did the same and were vulnerable sharing something personal with others.

Be prepared for these questions:
- How/Why does authenticity draw people closer?
- What keeps people from being authentic/vulnerable?
- When could being vulnerable be unwise or unsafe?
- How can authenticity be used in Coaching?

WEEK 3 | PEER MEETING

Week 3 Review
- Walk through the Authentic Sharing exercise together.
- Share highlights from the Metacognition project.
- Which of the coaching values from Chapter 6 did you choose to lean into and why?
- What is one thing you chose to talk about from the reading?

JOURNEYING
God Always Offers a Plan

We expect there to be messes in our homes. When stuff happens, our belief systems can falter if our life expectations don't have room for messes. Then our focus is on why there is stuff rather than on how to build a bridge.

Here are some of the things we think:
- I'm a Christian, so nothing bad should happen to me or to anyone I care about.
- This bad thing happened so I must have sin in my life.
- If God is so powerful, why did He allow this _____(accident, illness, difficulty, death...) to happen?
- God is absent/silent when I need Him most.
- The enemy has the upper hand in this situation.
- This wasn't supposed to happen.

God wants to be the hero, an active player in the story of our lives.

The following comes from a poem of unknown origin that was popularized by Corrie Ten Boom (author of *The Hiding Place*):

My Life is but a weaving
between my Lord and me;
I cannot choose the colors
He worketh steadily.

Oft times He weaveth sorrow
And I, in foolish pride,
Forget He sees the upper,
And I the under side.

Not til the loom is silent
And the shuttles cease to fly,
Shall God unroll the canvas
And explain the reason why.

The dark threads are as needful
In the Weaver's skillful hand,
As the threads of gold and silver
In the pattern He has planned.

He knows, He loves, He cares,
Nothing this truth can dim.
He gives His very best to those
Who leave the choice with Him.

What might God be doing in the midst of your mess?

_____

_____

_____

_____

_____

_____

_____

What might God be doing in the situations around you?

_____

_____

_____

_____

_____

_____

_____

What character quality is God trying to reveal about Himself in these situations?

_____

_____

_____

_____

_____

_____

_____

WEEK 4 COURSEWORK: ACTIVE LISTENING

- Focus Video
- Reading
- Online Discussion
- Project
- Peer Meeting

▶ WEEK 4 | FOCUS VIDEO

Watch the "Active Listening" videos.

WEEK 4 | READING: CHAPTERS 11 & 12

Note: These chapters are out of order but are the correct chapters dealing with the subject matter this week.

WEEK 4 | ONLINE DISCUSSION: HONEST REASONS WE DON'T LISTEN

In the Facebook group, work on a list together of why listening is so difficult.

Add at least three reasons to the list.

WEEK 4 | PROJECT: ACTIVE LISTENING

Plan at least two different conversations where you are intentionally listening. (Do this project after reading this week's chapters.)

Take some time afterward to record your thoughts on:
- What was most difficult as you intentionally focused on active listening?
- How did it work out?
- How do you think the other person felt?

_____

_____

_____

_____

_____

_____

In your normal conversations this week make it a point to notice if active listening is a common practice. Be prepared to share your thoughts.

👥 WEEK 4 | PEER MEETING

Week 4 Review
- Talk about your active listening experiences. What stands out to you?
- How does active listening fit the definition of Coaching or the Always Circle?
- What are your thoughts about the Chapter 11 title "Curiosity vs. Diagnosis"?

PERSONAL COACHING SESSION

This week will be your second personal coaching session. We'll talk about the action steps we settled on last time and move forward from there.

ACTIVE LISTENING
The Synergy of Trust and Caring Curiosity

WHY LISTEN AND NOT JUST TELL?

_____

_____

_____

_____

_____

> ᗡᗡᗡ
>
> **The best way to love someone is to listen to them.**
>
> **JOSHUA FINLEY**

Common Roles That Can Keep People from Listening
[Inspired by Lifeforming Leadership Coaching]

Interrupting Robber_____

_____

Comparing Historian_____

_____

Interrogating Judge_____

_____

Diagnosing Professional_____

_____

Commanding General_____

_____

Quick-Change Artist_____

_____

Talk Time
Get with a partner or two and answer this question:
Which of these would you most likely tend toward and why?

How to Listen Well

[Inspired by Transformissional Coaching by Steve Ogne, Tim Roehl and Ed Stetzer]

BE CURIOUS!

LET THEM LEAD.

"CLARIPHRASE" – repeat back to them what you think they are saying

DON'T BE AFRAID OF SILENCE.

LISTEN FOR "AHA," "UH OH," OR "HMMM…" MOMENTS

3 Levels of Listening

1) SELF-FOCUSED
- "What do I have in common with this experience?"

2) OTHERS-FOCUSED
- True curiosity and empathy

3) GOD-FOCUSED
- "What's really happening in the spiritual realm here?"
- "What character qualities does God want to reveal through this experience?"
- "What does the person need to go deeper?"

3 Types of Questions

OPEN QUESTIONS are driven by true care and curiosity
- "Tell me more about…"
- "What did that feel like?"
- "What is important about that?"

CLOSED QUESTIONS go nowhere, have one word answers, have right or wrong answers, and/or sound judgy.
- "Was that a right response?"
- "Did that make you feel bad?"
- "What were you thinking?"

LEADING QUESTIONS offer a solution in the form of a preferred suggestion.
- "Don't you think you should talk to him about that?"
- "Why don't you just set up a task list?"
- "You know what I would do?"

Asking open questions releases the coach from directing the conversation and leans into the leading of the Holy Spirit, trusting that God is always drawing people to alignment with Him!

Talk Time: *Active Listening*

1. Think of an area in your life where you would like forward movement. If you need a little help choose one of the following:
    - A habit that you would like to start or one you would like to stop
    - A hurt that has been holding you back
    - A conflict that needs to be resolved
    - A dream you would like to pursue

2. Get with a partner and take turns listening to each other (split the time in half equally).

3. The only rules are that you cannot offer your resolution or share your stories but only ask them for more information. If you don't resolve the entire situation in a few minutes, don't worry! It will likely take more time. Just offer a true listening and trusting heart.

    Try a sequence of phrases like this:
    "What would you like to talk about today?"
    "What's on your mind?"
    "What would a 'win' look like in that area?"
    "If this situation were resolved or that new goal were accomplished, what would that be like?"
    "Why is this important?"

Journal Time

Take some time to record your thoughts about your active listening exercise.

What was most difficult as you intentionally focused on active listening?

_____

_____

_____

_____

How do you think you did?

_____

_____

_____

_____

_____

How do you think the other person felt?

_____

_____

_____

_____

How did you feel?

_____

_____

_____

_____

Listening is caring. People can resolve much if they are simply given the chance to verbalize without interruption.

One-Minute Takeaway
Take one minute to write down what stood out to you in this session.

_____

_____

_____

_____

_____

_____

BRIDGES COACHING

Coaching Session   Date: _____

Focus:_____
_____
_____

Coaching Appointment Notes:_____
_____
_____
_____
_____
_____
_____
_____

Action Steps for Next Coaching Appointment:

☐ _____
☐ _____
☐ _____
☐ _____
☐ _____

Concerns or Challenges:_____
_____
_____
_____
_____
_____
_____

NEXT APPOINTMENT   Date: _____   Time: _____

Coach Form

BRIDGES COACHING

Client Name: _____   Date: _____

Client Progress Report:_____

_____

_____

_____

_____

_____

_____

_____

Focus:_____

_____

_____

Coaching Appointment Notes: _____

_____

_____

_____

_____

_____

_____

Action Steps for Next Coaching Appointment:_____

_____

_____

_____

_____

_____

NEXT APPOINTMENT   Date: _____   Time: _____

BRIDGES COACHING

COACHING EVALUATION

Assess the coaching session you observed.

Coaching Asssessment

What percentage of the time was the coachee talking? _____

What was the goal of the client? _____

_____

_____

What was the most powerful question? _____

_____

What would you say was the strong suit in this session? _____

_____

_____

What action step(s) were agreed upon?

_____

_____

_____

_____

_____

_____

_____

Any questions you have:

_____

_____

_____

_____

_____

- Focus Video
- Reading
- Online Discussion
- Project
- Prep for Peer Meeting
- Peer Meeting
- Preparation for Class

▶ WEEK 5 | FOCUS VIDEO

Watch the "Asking Powerful Questions" videos.
(Bonus Video Available: "Top Ten Things Coaching is NOT and Intro to ROAD," these topics will be covered in the mid-point group class.)

📚 WEEK 5 | READING: CHAPTER 13

Do Exercise 13.3 (in white) and 13.5. Be prepared to discuss in peer meeting.

Consider the other exercises and pick another if you'd like.

💬 WEEK 5 | ONLINE DISCUSSION: HONEST REASONS WE TAKE CONTROL

Let's build a list together. Add three reasons why we want to take control.

⚙ WEEK 5 | PROJECT: ASKING WITH INTEREST - MINING FOR MEANING

Plan and have at least two half-hour coaching conversations where your focus is to practice asking powerful questions without an agenda mindset. Get curious, let of go control.

Write your thoughts on the next page. Be prepared to talk about your experiences.

_____

_____

_____

_____

_____

_____

_____

_____

_____

_____

_____

 ## WEEK 5 | PEER MEETING

Week 5 Review
- Debrief Exercise 13.3 (in white) and 13.5.
- Process "Asking Powerful Questions" Conversations.
- Brainstorm ideas to let go of control and to develop trust.

 ## WEEK 5 | PREPARATION FOR CLASS

Be prepared to share this finished sentence with the class:
- One thing I love about coaching so far is _____.

Bring results of Exercise 8.4 to class (see Week 6 Reading). You may want to start this early.

ASKING POWERFUL QUESTIONS
The Art of Agenda-free Interest

WHAT IS A POWERFUL QUESTION?

A powerful question is one that provides:
- a perspective that was not clear before the question. "That's a good question."
- an "aha," "uh oh," or "hmm…" moment.
- clarity on an issue, an obstacle or a goal. "I never thought of that."

Possible Characteristics of a Powerful Question

- An ask to go deeper
- Mirroring and/or release of emotion
- Thinking things through logically
- Options not considered before
- Addressing an obstacle

_____

_____

_____

_____

_____

_____

_____

_____

_____

_____

_____

_____

_____

_____

What Makes a Question Not So Powerful?

One with an agenda
- "Do you know how to use Google calendar?"
  - Better: "What could you use to keep track of your schedule?"
  - Best: "What are your options?"

A back door tell
- "Many women have read this book. Would you like to borrow mine?"
  - Better: "Would a book be a good resource for you?"
  - Best: "Where could you get more information?"

Anything with a right or wrong answer
- "Was it right to talk to him that way?"
  - Better: "Looking back at the situation now, what would you do differently?"
  - Bigger: "Tell me more about what was going on inside you."

Something that is informational instead of transformational
- "Do you think you need to research that?"
  - Better: "Would it be helpful to take a deeper look?"
  - Bigger: "What's next?"

A question that is shallow
- "Did that make you sad?"
  - Better: "What were some of the things going on inside you when that happened?"
  - Bigger: "Tell me more."

A diagnosis
- "Is that lie based?"
  - Better: "If there were a lie in there what would it be?"
  - Bigger: "What's going on inside?"

The NICE Model for Asking Powerful Questions
NOTICE - INQUIRE - CHOOSE - EVALUATE

NOTICE TOOL: CURIOSITY TRIGGERS

Emotional response - may be noticed by a physical or verbal cue that there is more going on.

- Tremor in the voice
- Pause in speaking
- Tears
- Sighing
- Jiggling feet or legs
- Crossed arms
- An eye roll
- Lip biting
- Stronger than normal reaction

Repetition
- When the client uses certain verbiage repeatedly, be sure to repeat the exact words back or ask for clarification.
- Bringing up a certain situation more than once can be a clue that it is not yet resolved.

Statements of possible intention
- "Probably should..."
- "I ought to..."

Counsel
- Someone else has given advice to them.
- Feeling like God has directed their steps.

Patterns
- Bringing up something similar that was resolved positively or negatively in the past.
- Mentions an experience that resembles something they have already been through.

Concerns
- Is there anything that is questionable or unbiblical?
- Are there themes that are making you wonder?
- Are there things that make you concerned or uncomfortable?

Talk Time

Which one of these will be easiest for you to notice, and which will be most difficult?

_____

_____

_____

_____

_____

Emotional Response
"I noticed that you (insert physical response here – like "teared up there") is that something we should talk about?"

Repetition
"You mentioned _____ a number of times. Can you tell me more about that?"

Statements of Possible Intention
"I noted you said you probably ought to _____. Can you tell me what is holding you back from moving on there?"

Counsel
(Others) "You mentioned _____ said maybe you ought to _____. How do you feel about that?"
(God) "You mentioned that you felt like God wanted you to _____. How can you make a step toward saying yes to that?" or "What is holding you back from moving forward there?"

Patterns
"I'm wondering if there may be a pattern. Do you think _____ and _____ (and _____) could be related? If so, what would be the connections? If not, how are they not similar?"

Concerns
"I just need to put this on the table. I'm wondering if _____ needs to be addressed."
"I'm not comfortable with _____. Can we talk about that?"
"What am I missing that _____ seems to be okay?"
"I'm wondering if we need to redirect and talk about _____."

✎ Journal Time

What are a couple of the question starters that you could easily see becoming a part of your regular vocabulary?

_____

_____

_____

_____

_____

CHOICE TOOL: DECISION CONSIDERATIONS

- **Moral/Biblical Issues** - Boundaries
- **Timing**
- **Readiness or Willingness**
- **Ownership**

Talk Time
What will be the most difficult part of allowing the other person to lead?

_____

_____

_____

_____

_____

EVALUATION TOOL: REVISITING TECHNIQUES

_____

_____

_____

_____

_____

_____

_____

Group Share
How can we re-approach any area that we have a concern in without pushing our own agenda?

_____

_____

_____

_____

_____

✏️ Journal Time

Take some time and consider two situations where you need to use the coaching approach. Write your thoughts below.

_____
_____
_____
_____
_____
_____
_____
_____
_____
_____

How could using Powerful Questions help people move forward in a more effective way than telling them what to do or avoiding them?

_____
_____
_____
_____
_____
_____
_____
_____
_____
_____

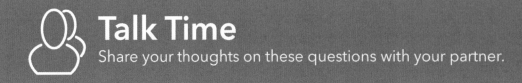

Talk Time
Share your thoughts on these questions with your partner.

- ☐ **Reading**
- ☐ **Peer Meeting**
- ☐ **Group Class**
- ☐ **Online Discussion**

 ## WEEK 6 | READING: CHAPTERS 7 & 8

Do Exercise 8.1. Be prepared to share in your peer meeting this week.

Do Exercise 8.4. See file in Facebook group this week for a prototype of the Bridges Coaching Welcome Letter and Packet, bring completed excersize to class.

 ## WEEK 6 | PEER MEETING

Week 6 Review
- Share thoughts about see/say principle (see page 96).
- Share your 60-second thoughts from Exercise 8.1.
- Discuss options for coaching practicum. Ask client/volunteer to your peer meeting at specific times.

PERSONAL COACHING

This week will be your third personal coaching session. We'll talk about the action steps we settled on last time and move forward from there.

 ## WEEK 6 | GROUP CLASS

Reconnect. Each trainee will share the ending to the sentence "One thing I love about coaching so far is _____."

Coaching Recap and Intro to the Coaching ROAD.

WEEK 6 | ONLINE DISCUSSION: SUCCESS EQUALS AN ACTIVE
RELATIONSHIP WITH GOD

- What are the more "normal" ways to measure success?
- How do these differ from the typical definition of success?
- What does success look like in the Kingdom?

Share your thoughts and reply to at least 2 other posts.

TOP TEN THINGS
COACHING IS *NOT*

#10 COACHING IS NOT _____

 #9 COACHING IS NOT _____

 #8 COACHING IS NOT _____

 #7 COACHING IS NOT _____

 #6 COACHING IS NOT _____

 #5 COACHING IS NOT _____

 #4 COACHING IS NOT _____

 #3 COACHING IS NOT _____

 #2 COACHING IS NOT _____

 #1 COACHING IS NOT _____

Leaders have 3 bottomline choices...

1) THEY CAN _____ PEOPLE.

2) THEY CAN _____ PEOPLE.

3) THEY CAN HELP THEM _____ AND WISELY _____ THEIR OWN PATH.

✎ Journal Time

Without the coaching paradigm, which would you most tend toward—carrying or pushing people?

_____

_____

Talk Time
Which of the Top Ten Things Coaching Is Not is the most powerful to you and why?

FOCUS
The Power of Goals in Transformation

Success equals an ACTIVE RELATIONSHIP with God!

REASONS WHY INTENTIONAL LIVING IS GODLY
Why to Not Just "See How it Goes"

_____

_____

_____

_____

_____

_____

TRANSFORMATION = (Repentance) CHANGE YOUR HEART
+
CHANGE YOUR LIFE

FOCUS IS IMPORTANT BECAUSE IT PROVIDES A GOAL.

It can be difficult to get a person to the place of focusing on a goal, but if they can't focus it may be impossible to help them. You may only be dealing with the circumstances and issues but not with people who are growing and living intentionally.

GPS only works if you know the address!

Think of a reoccurring coversation

_____

TYPICAL SCENARIOS OF THE UNFOCUSED

The _____ talks and talks about everything and has multiple issues.
The _____ just wants to dump emotional baggage because it gives momentary relief.
The _____ is convinced their circumstance is extraordinary and they cannot be expected to overcome.

Go back to your recurring conversation. Which of the characters above fits the situation? How would having a focus or goal change the conversation?

_____

_____

_____

_____

What is a question that would focus the conversation toward a healthy end?

_____

_____

_____

_____

COACHING

As coaches, our first tasks are to:
- Believe God has us all on an amazing journey.
- Help our coachee to recognize:
  - where they are,
  - where they want to go,
  - what obstacles are keeping them from forward movement,
  - what the next step is.

Coaches start with "here" and move to "there."
- Here is "who I am" and "what I am doing."
- There is "who He made me to be" and "what He has for me to do."

THE BRIDGES COACHING ROAD

R - Recognition
O - Ownership
A - Action
D - Dedication

BRIDGES COACHING

Coaching Session   Date: _____

Focus:_____

_____

_____

Coaching Appointment Notes: _____

_____

_____

_____

_____

_____

_____

_____

Action Steps for Next Coaching Appointment:

☐ _____

☐ _____

☐ _____

☐ _____

☐ _____

Concerns or Challenges:_____

_____

_____

_____

_____

_____

_____

NEXT APPOINTMENT   Date: _____   Time: _____

Coach Form

BRIDGES COACHING

Client Name: _____   Date: _____

Client Progress Report:_____

_____

_____

_____

_____

_____

_____

_____

_____

Focus:_____

_____

_____

Coaching Appointment Notes:_____

_____

_____

_____

_____

_____

_____

Action Steps for Next Coaching Appointment:_____

_____

_____

_____

_____

_____

NEXT APPOINTMENT   Date: _____   Time: _____

BRIDGES COACHING

COACHING EVALUATION

Assess the coaching session you observed.

Coaching Asssessment

What percentage of the time was the coachee talking? _____

What was the goal of the client? _____

_____

_____

What was the most powerful question? _____

_____

What would you say was the strong suit in this session? _____

_____

_____

What action step(s) were agreed upon?

_____

_____

_____

_____

_____

_____

_____

Any questions you have:

_____

_____

_____

_____

_____

Additional Resource:
The Power of Focus by Jack Canfield, Mark Victor Hansen, and Les Hewitt

- Focus Video
- Project
- Reading
- Online Discussion
- Project
- Peer Meeting
- Coaching Evaluation

▶ WEEK 7 | FOCUS VIDEO

Watch the "Recognition" videos.

⚙ WEEK 7 | PROJECT: PROCESSING FILTERS

Project included in video teaching notes.

📚 WEEK 7 | READING: CHAPTER 9

Which of the seven ways to keep the client in charge intrigued you the most and why?

_____

_____

_____

_____

💬 WEEK 7 | ONLINE DISCUSSION: RECOGNITION

Part 1: What keeps people from recognizing or focusing?
Make a list of things that keep people from focusing. Share an original thought (try not to say the same thing as the people who have posted before you.)

Part 2: What are some ideas you can use to help people realize the value of focus?
Reply to the thoughts listed in Part 1 with ideas that may help. Reply to at least two posts.

WEEK 7 | PROJECT: WELCOME LETTER

Send your prepared welcome letter to your volunteer client prior to your Peer Meeting this week.

WEEK 7 | PEER MEETING

Review Week 7
- Which of the seven ways to keep the client in charge did you choose and why?
- Share one thought from the processing filters project.
- 1st Coaching Practicum pre-brief
  - Be cautious not to use run-on questions.
  - Don't feel pressure to drive- listen, be curious and let client lead.
  - Take care to watch the time so you don't need to rush at the end- start the close about 10 minutes out.
  - Ask them what they have written for action steps.

COACHING PRACTICUM

This week will be your initial coaching session. You will walk your client through the Welcome Packet and set initial goals.

Recognition

R - Recognition
O - Ownership
A - Action
D - Dedication

Clarity is currently a buzzword in both ministry and the marketplace, for good reason. Knowing where to focus gives us clarity to work toward a specific target. If you don't know your destination, it will be hard to find your pathway.

3 Ways to Recognize a Focus Area

If you are not sure what you're shooting for, it will be difficult to aim!

1) DREAM DEVELOPMENT

Hopes/Dreams are promptings from God. He seeds ideas within you that He wants to grow. This is likely the easiest focus to determine as you already know it. It has been in your heart.

_____

_____

_____

_____

_____

_____

_____

2) DECIDE LIFE ASSESSMENT - WHEEL OF LIFE

A wheel tool is used to assess life satisfaction and recognize any possible blind spots. There can be areas in life that need attention, and a wheel can save people from possible neglect.

As you consider each spoke of the Bridges Coaching Tree/Wheel of Life, assign a number from 1-10 (1 being lowest, 10 highest) to each area that reflects your personal satisfaction in your connection with God's will for your life in this area for this season. Be cautious not to compare yourself with someone else's norm, but rather with however you feel you are connecting with God's will for you in that area.

_____ WORSHIP is your connection to a local church and corporate worship. How do you feel about your connection with the body of believers God has led you to?

_____ MISSIONS is your involvement with reaching out beyond local connections. How do you feel about your praying, giving, and going in the missions arena?

_____ VOLUNTEERING in the church with your unique design and place in the body. Are you engaged at the level God is asking you to be in at your local church?

_____ FELLOWSHIP is a smaller group of people that you are doing life with. Are you in a small group? Do you have a close circle of friends that you live life with?

_____ FAMILY is connection with parents, children, and spouse and/or significant other. Do you feel this area needs more focus?

_____ PERSONAL CARE AND DEVELOPMENT is stewardship of your physical body, your emotional well-being, life-learning, or whatever area you are feeling drawn to. Are you aligned with God's plan for your personal care and development?

_____ DEVOTIONAL LIFE is caring for your own spirit by connecting with God and His word. How do you feel about your investment level in your roots?

_____ INTENTIONAL LIVING is your pace of life and focus. Are you running your life or is your life running you? Consider your financial situation as well. Are you controlling your money or is your money controlling you?

_____ HOUSEHOLD is your level of comfort in your home. Are there things you should be focused on to make your home a sanctuary?

_____ OUTREACH CONNECTIONS are your involvements with people who are pre-Christians. Are you content with your level of interactions outside Christian circles?

_____ HOBBIES/RECREATION is what you do to relax. How do you feel about your level of release to feed your soul in this way?

_____ WORK is your career or contribution to society. Are you satisfied with your connection with your God-given role for this season of your life? Are you being the best you in the best place possible for the majority of your work week?

When you are finished, fill in the corresponding spoke to the ring that matches. (Each line from the center is worth 2 points on a 1-10 scale.) Your finished wheel will look something like this.

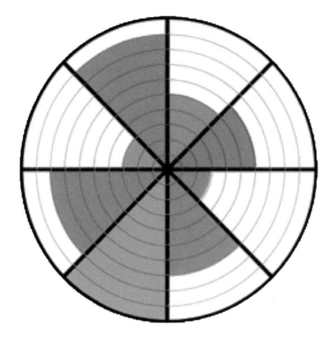

When you are finished with your wheel assessment, take some time to consider the lower spokes of your wheel.

Pray about which one, or two, you feel God is asking you to focus on at this time. Maybe choose character qualities to work on; some examples could be releasing fear, or becoming more patient. You can also choose physical things like weight loss or redecorating. Or you may want relational goals like improving your relationship with your spouse or friends. The point is that you work with God on the next step in your personal journey.

What would it take for you to feel like you had a "win" in that area?

_____

_____

_____

_____

_____

3) DRILLING DOWN A FOCAL POINT

_____

_____

_____

_____

Which of the 3 ways will you utilize to choose your focus?

_____

In one sentence, what are you going to recognize as the destination for your ROAD coaching exercise?

_____

_____

_____

Why is focusing on this goal important?

_____

_____

_____

_____

What will happen if you don't change, grow, or achieve this goal?

_____

_____

_____

_____

What will you and others gain if you do achieve it?

_____

_____

_____

_____

_____

7 Filters to Processing God's Voice

PROCESSING GOD'S VOICE

The checkpoints to knowing God's voice are important. These checkpoints will aid in the prevention of a "God card" mentality.

Ever been with someone who tells you, "God told me to _____ (insert random goal here)." Or maybe you have been the person saying it?

1) _____ IN YOUR OWN HEART / _____ TOWARD THE IDEA

_____

_____

2) _____ OF SCRIPTURE

_____

_____

3) _____

_____

_____

4) _____ OR LEADERS

_____

_____

5) _____ OR SPOUSE

_____

6) _____

_____

_____

7) _____ - CIRCUMSTANCES OR TIMING

_____

_____

Taking a goal through the filters will enhance its clarity and reveal its flow.

God offers clarity through the wisdom of checkpoints.

Consider the filters listed as P's.
- Peace in own heart
- Passages of scripture
- Parents
- Pastors or leaders
- Partner/spouse
- Peers
- Particulars - circumstances, timing

Which of these areas has been a strong suit in your life?

_____

_____

Are any of these a new thought to you? If so, which one(s) and how could you lean into them more?

_____

_____

Who are some individuals you could approach in each of the relational areas? (Parents/spiritual parents; pastors or leaders; peers)

_____

_____

Consider how God has used the particulars to guide you in at least one area in your past and write your thoughts here.

_____

_____

_____

_____

What is one of the filter areas God may want you to lean into at this time in your life? How could you say yes to Him and do that?

_____

_____

_____

How could a coaching leader use this teaching without being a "teller"?

_____

_____

_____

BRIDGES COACHING

Coaching Session   Date: _____

Focus:_____

_____

_____

Coaching Appointment Notes:_____

_____

_____

_____

_____

_____

_____

_____

Action Steps for Next Coaching Appointment:

_____

_____

_____

_____

_____

_____

Concerns or Challenges:_____

_____

_____

_____

_____

_____

_____

NEXT APPOINTMENT   Date: _____   Time: _____

BRIDGES COACHING

Coach Form

Client Name: _____   Date: _____

Client Progress Report: _____

_____

_____

_____

_____

_____

_____

_____

Focus: _____

_____

_____

Coaching Appointment Notes: _____

_____

_____

_____

_____

_____

_____

Action Steps for Next Coaching Appointment: _____

_____

_____

_____

_____

_____

NEXT APPOINTMENT   Date: _____   Time: _____

BRIDGES COACHING

COACHING EVALUATION

Assess the coaching session you observed.

Coaching Asssessment

What percentage of the time was the coachee talking? _____

What was the goal of the client? _____
_____
_____

What was the most powerful question? _____
_____

What would you say was the strong suit in this session? _____
_____
_____

What action step(s) were agreed upon?
_____
_____
_____
_____
_____
_____
_____

Any questions you have:
_____
_____
_____
_____
_____

BRIDGES COACHING

Coaching Session   Date: _____

Focus:_____

_____

_____

Coaching Appointment Notes: _____

_____

_____

_____

_____

_____

_____

_____

_____

Action Steps for Next Coaching Appointment:

☐ _____

☐ _____

☐ _____

☐ _____

☐ _____

Concerns or Challenges:_____

_____

_____

_____

_____

_____

_____

NEXT APPOINTMENT   Date: _____   Time: _____

Coach Form

BRIDGES COACHING

Client Name: _____   Date: _____

Client Progress Report: _____

_____

_____

_____

_____

_____

_____

_____

Focus: _____

_____

_____

Coaching Appointment Notes: _____

_____

_____

_____

_____

_____

_____

Action Steps for Next Coaching Appointment: _____

_____

_____

_____

_____

_____

NEXT APPOINTMENT   Date: _____   Time: _____

BRIDGES COACHING

COACHING EVALUATION

Assess the coaching session you observed.

Coaching Asssessment

What percentage of the time was the coachee talking? _____

What was the goal of the client? _____
_____
_____

What was the most powerful question? _____
_____

What would you say was the strong suit in this session? _____
_____
_____

What action step(s) were agreed upon?
_____
_____
_____
_____
_____
_____
_____

Any questions you have:
_____
_____
_____
_____
_____

WEEK 8 COURSEWORK:
O - OWNERSHIP

- ☐ **Focus Video**
- ☐ **Journal Time**
- ☐ **Project**
- ☐ **Reading**
- ☐ **Online Discussion**
- ☐ **Peer Meeting**

Additional Resource:
The Power of Focus by Jack Canfield, Mark Victor Hansen, and Les Hewitt

▶ **WEEK 8 | FOCUS VIDEO:**

Watch the "Ownership" videos.

 WEEK 8 | JOURNAL TIME: OWNERSHIP

Process and/or focus journal times as directed in video.

 WEEK 8 | PROJECT: FREEDOM PRAYER

See prompts from the "Ownership" video regarding the Freedom Prayer.

📚 **WEEK 8 | READING:** CHAPTER 15

Do Exercise 15.4.

 WEEK 8 | ONLINE DISCUSSION:
DEALING WITH AVOIDERS WITHOUT BEING A TELLER

In the online discussion think of a real situation in your own life or of someone who shares their life with you and write one powerful question that could help someone take ownership for their life.

WEEK 8 | PEER MEETING

Review Week 8
- Review Exercise 15.4.
- Share something from the Freedom Prayer exercise.

PERSONAL COACHING SESSION

This week will be your final personal coaching session. We'll talk about the progress you made and what you need to move forward toward your goal and live intentionally.

OWNERSHIP

_____

_____

_____

_____

_____

_____

Ownership is saying no one can do anything about this except me. I am who I am and this "stuff" is my own. My circumstances do not own me. I am who I choose to be.

OBSTACLES THAT KEEP US FROM OWNERSHIP

Blame

Excuses

Procrastination

Apathy

Minimizing

Fear

Doubt

Other – _____

✏ Journal Time

Which one of these could be the one affecting you most at this time?

_____

_____

_____

_____

_____

_____

_____

_____

False Hopes = "Deliverance" will come from somewhere else

IF ONLY... (PAST, PRESENT, FUTURE)

Past

- I had different parents.
- I had grown up in a different church with better _____.
- I hadn't missed out on _____.
- I had exposure to _____.
- That hadn't happened. (abuse, words, sickness or disease, lack, event...)

Present

- I wasn't dealing with _____.
- I had more money.
- I had more time.
- I wasn't _____.
- I knew _____.
- Someone would reach out to me.
- My church had a better program.
- I would get to the right event or knew the right seminar to go to.
- I could wait a little longer.

Future

- I could get an appointment with a certain person.
- I could afford professional counseling.
- I could find the right book.
- I made more money so I could _____.
- I had a boyfriend/girlfriend/spouse.
- Something amazing would happen: an inheritance, a healing, winning the lottery, getting noticed by "somebody"...

No one and nothing can own your life unless you allow it. God made a way for you to move forward even through obstacles. The only obstacle you have to overcome is your own will.

✏ Journal Time

If you had to pick a false hope as your primary "go to," which one would it be?

_____

_____

_____

_____

Facts & Feelings. Lies & Truth.

Write win here:
(ie. I will live in freedom... or I will move forward in my dream of ...)

_____

_____

_____

The following pathway assists in removing the skewed view:

- Think of a situation where you have dealt with this lie
- Identify the facts and the feelings you are dealing with.
- Write out the lie in sentence form.
- Take it to Jesus and repent for choosing to believe that lie.
- Forgive those who contributed to your acceptance of that lie.
- Ask for release from any attachments with darkness associated with the lie. Take your time considering how believing this lie has affected you.. (ex. depression, anxiety, anger…)
- Request a truth to be revealed to take the place of the lie.
- Consider ways to refocus your new vision.
- Talk about it. Share your experience with at least one person, or preferably with more. The more you talk about it the more real the truth becomes for you.
- Make a plan to revisit this concept on a regular basis. This can be a kind of scheduled self check-up.

Freedom Prayer

Father, I can see now that I have believed the lie that _____ . I no longer choose to live my life or base my thoughts on this lie.

Please forgive me for choosing to make this lie a part of who I am and basing my thoughts on it. I forgive everyone who has contributed to my thinking this way. (List as needed.)

Jesus has already won the victory so I claim freedom from any attachments with darkness due to this lie. (List as needed.) Help me to break my thought patterns and any lifestyle choices connected with this lie. Help me to see how it has affected me and then help me instead to be conformed to be like Christ.

As I live my new life in Christ, I will now believe the truth that _____. My new mindset will include these views. (Ask God for new values statements and new attachments and list them.)

The word of my testimony will be how You set me free!

✏️ Journal Time

Take a lie you have recognized and walk through these steps.

Incident:_____

_____

Facts & Feelings:_____

_____

Lie: _____

_____

I repend of choosing to believe this lie and viewing life through this lens.

I forgive:_____

_____

I renounce:_____

_____

Truth:_____

_____

New Values:_____

_____

New Foci:_____

_____

Ways to refocus:_____

_____

People to talk to:_____

_____

Plan to revisit:_____

_____

BRIDGES COACHING

Coaching Session   Date: _____

Focus:_____

_____

_____

Coaching Appointment Notes: _____

_____

_____

_____

_____

_____

_____

_____

Action Steps for Next Coaching Appointment:

☐ _____

☐ _____

☐ _____

☐ _____

☐ _____

Concerns or Challenges:_____

_____

_____

_____

_____

_____

_____

NEXT APPOINTMENT   Date: _____   Time: _____

Coach Form

BRIDGES COACHING

Client Name: _____   Date: _____

Client Progress Report: _____

_____

_____

_____

_____

_____

_____

_____

Focus: _____

_____

_____

Coaching Appointment Notes: _____

_____

_____

_____

_____

_____

_____

Action Steps for Next Coaching Appointment:_____

_____

_____

_____

_____

_____

NEXT APPOINTMENT   Date: _____   Time: _____

BRIDGES COACHING

COACHING EVALUATION

Assess the coaching session you observed.

Coaching Asssessment

What percentage of the time was the coachee talking? _____

What was the goal of the client? _____
_____
_____

What was the most powerful question? _____
_____

What would you say was the strong suit in this session? _____
_____
_____

What action step(s) were agreed upon?
_____
_____
_____
_____
_____
_____
_____
_____

Any questions you have:
_____
_____
_____
_____
_____

- Focus Video
- Reading
- Project
- Online Discussion
- Peer Meeting/Coaching Practicum 2nd Session

▶ WEEK 9 | FOCUS VIDEO

Watch the "Action Steps" videos.

WEEK 9 | READING: CHAPTER 10

WEEK 9 | PROJECT: SMART GOALS

Work through the SMART goal projects as laid out in the focus video.

WEEK 9 | ONLINE DISCUSSION: ACTION STEPS

WEEK 9 | PEER MEETING

Review Week 9
- Share one result of your SMART goal project.
- Any questions or thoughts in this area?
- How could adding action steps change a regular conversation into a coaching one?
- Brainstorm how you could add action steps in a casual conversation.
- 2nd Coaching Practicum pre-breif:
  - Be cautious not to follow up too strong on action steps (judgy) or be too soft by not bringing them up at all if the client doesn't mention them.
  - Don't forget to allow for a possible change in focus or drill down on an obstacle before moving forward.

COACHING PRACTICUM

This week will be your second coaching session. Talk with your client about their action steps and see where they want to go next.

ACTION STEPS

_____

_____

_____

_____

_____

SMART Goals

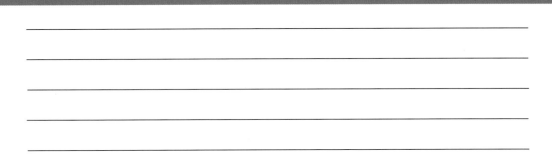

SMART Goals
S - SPECIFIC
M - MEASURABLE
A - ATTAINABLE
R - RELEVANT
T - TIME-SENSITIVE

SPECIFIC - A specific goal is described clearly to others. You know what you want to accomplish. Vague goals equate to vague results. Smart goals must be fully furnished with detailed description of the what, when, and how.

MEASURABLE - A goal is measurable when you can clearly define what it means to reach it. You can assess your progress. Goals which cannot be measured cannot be managed. Your goal is measurable if anyone can tell you at the end of the deadline, whether or not you have completed your goal.

ATTAINABLE - Your goal must be within your reach in your present situation. High goals that stretch you are okay, but high and realistic goals are better. Unattainable goals do not motivate you. Easy goals, on the other hand, are not challenging enough. They do not contribute to your growth.

RELEVANT - Goals need to be parallel to your purpose in life. Relevant goals are a sure way to direct your efforts towards attaining something that is focused on where you are directing attention. Goals are simply instruments to accomplishing one's mission/purpose in life.

TIME-SENSITIVE - Goals need to have deadlines. A goal free from time element is susceptible to procrastination.

The key is to be specific.

1) BREAK IT DOWN INTO WEEKLY GOALS.
2) SET UP ACCOUNTABILITY.
3) REVISIT AS NEEDED.

SMART GOALS

Take your focus area and walk through these questions. Build your own SMART goal. (See below for examples of finished SMART goals.) For practice, time permitting feel free to work through someone else's SMART goals.

Specific: What specifically will I achieve?
Measurable: How will I measure it?
Attainable: Is it achievable now?
Relevant: Is it relevant to my larger goals?
Time-sensitive: By what dates will I achieve it?

Examples

- I will lose 10 lbs by my birthday, starting by working out 2 times a week and not eating sugar. I'll reassess my progress and make adjustments as needed to achieve my goal.
- I will work through my fear of people and be able to talk to strangers by the New Year's Eve party. I'll start small and work up to cold contact greeting.
- I will work through my anger issue and be able to turn my reactions into responses by the end of the school year. I'll work through each heated interaction with my coach and learn to discern healthy options.

_____
_____
_____
_____

Now, let's break it down:

What is your weekly goal?

_____
_____
_____

How will you invite accountability?

_____
_____
_____

When will you revisit?

_____
_____
_____

BRIDGES COACHING

Coaching Session   Date: _____

Focus: _____

_____

_____

Coaching Appointment Notes: _____

_____

_____

_____

_____

_____

_____

_____

Action Steps for Next Coaching Appointment:

☐ _____

☐ _____

☐ _____

☐ _____

☐ _____

Concerns or Challenges: _____

_____

_____

_____

_____

_____

_____

NEXT APPOINTMENT   Date: _____   Time: _____

BRIDGES COACHING

Coach Form

Client Name: _____   Date: _____

Client Progress Report: _____

_____

_____

_____

_____

_____

_____

_____

Focus: _____

_____

_____

Coaching Appointment Notes: _____

_____

_____

_____

_____

_____

_____

Action Steps for Next Coaching Appointment: _____

_____

_____

_____

_____

_____

NEXT APPOINTMENT   Date: _____   Time: _____

BRIDGES COACHING

Coaching Session   Date: _____

Focus:_____

_____

_____

Coaching Appointment Notes: _____

_____

_____

_____

_____

_____

_____

_____

Action Steps for Next Coaching Appointment:

☐ _____

☐ _____

☐ _____

☐ _____

☐ _____

Concerns or Challenges:_____

_____

_____

_____

_____

_____

_____

NEXT APPOINTMENT   Date: _____   Time: _____

BRIDGES COACHING

COACHING EVALUATION

Assess the coaching session you observed.

Coaching Asssessment

What percentage of the time was the coachee talking? _____

What was the goal of the client? _____
_____
_____

What was the most powerful question? _____
_____

What would you say was the strong suit in this session? _____
_____
_____

What action step(s) were agreed upon?
_____
_____
_____
_____
_____
_____
_____

Any questions you have:
_____
_____
_____
_____
_____

BRIDGES COACHING

Coach Form

Client Name: _____ Date: _____

Client Progress Report: _____

_____

_____

_____

_____

_____

_____

_____

Focus: _____

_____

_____

Coaching Appointment Notes: _____

_____

_____

_____

_____

_____

Action Steps for Next Coaching Appointment: _____

_____

_____

_____

_____

_____

NEXT APPOINTMENT   Date: _____   Time: _____

BRIDGES COACHING

COACHING EVALUATION

Assess the coaching session you observed.

Coaching Asssessment

What percentage of the time was the coachee talking? _____

What was the goal of the client? _____
_____
_____

What was the most powerful question? _____
_____

What would you say was the strong suit in this session? _____
_____
_____

What action step(s) were agreed upon?
_____
_____
_____
_____
_____
_____
_____

Any questions you have:
_____
_____
_____
_____
_____

- ☐ **Focus Video**
- ☐ **Project**
- ☐ **Reading**
- ☐ **Online Discussion**
- ☐ **Peer Meeting**

▶ WEEK 10 | VIDEO

Watch the "Dedication" videos.

⚙ WEEK 10 | PROJECTS: DEDICATION

Do the Input & Evaluation Projects associated with the Dedication Videos.

📚 WEEK 10 | READING: CHAPTER 14

- Do Exercises 14.1, 14.2, 14.3.
- Be prepared to talk about "the box" you may be facing in your life.
- Consider doing 14.7 and 14.7 #2.

💬 WEEK 10 | ONLINE DISCUSSION: ENGAGING FEEDBACK

- Write a paragraph about feedback explaining how do people in your circles feel about it and include one idea that could be done to improve engaging input in our culture.
- Reply to at least two other posts.

👥 WEEK 10 | PEER MEETING

Review Week 10
- Share any thoughts about the Dedication Video.
- Debrief the Dedication projects.
- Talk about exercises 14.1, 14.2 and 14.3 and "the box" in your life.
- Check out the Powerful Questions examples together (see pages 223-227).

_____

_____

_____

_____

_____

Maintaining the Gain

Two ways to keep what you have worked for:
1) INPUT

_____

_____

_____

_____

_____

✏ Journal Time

Who should you be asking for input in your life? Consider 360° input spherically!

_____

_____

_____

When should you get input? Annually, each semester, monthly?

_____

_____

_____

How will you go about asking for information—an email, a survey, a chat?

_____

_____

What exactly do I want to ask? Write out your own question(s) here.

_____

_____

_____

_____

_____

2) EVALUATION

_____

_____

_____

_____

_____

✏ Journal Time

Determine your own yellow and red flags. Answer the following questions.

Decide how you define your own personal yellow and red flags.

_____

_____

_____

_____

Sketch out a personal plan for how and when you will check your progress.

_____

_____

_____

_____

- [ ] **Focus Video**
- [ ] **Project**
- [ ] **Focus Video**
- [ ] **Project**
- [ ] **Online Discussion**
- [ ] **Reading**
- [ ] **Focus Video**
- [ ] **Project**
- [ ] **Peer Prep**
- [ ] **Peer Meeting**

Additional Resource:
The Heart of Coaching
by Thomas Crane
Boundaries
by Cloud and Townsend

WEEK 11 | FOCUS VIDEO

Watch the "Support Pendulum" video.

WEEK 11 | PROJECT: SUPPORT PENDULUM EXERCISE

Do Support Pendulum Exercise associated with support video notes.

WEEK 11 | FOCUS VIDEO

Watch the "Boundaries" video.

WEEK 11 | PROJECT: BOUNDARIES EXERCISE

Follow Journal Prompts found in the Boundaries video.

WEEK 11 | ONLINE DISCUSSION:
ASSESSMENT OF EXCESS OR NEGLECT

Pick two current situations in your life where someone is looking to you for input or support.
Review the Excess and Neglect charts and consider where you are in each one. Are there any
adjustments that you need to make? Take your thoughts to the Discussion forum for this week.
(no names please)

Reply to at least two other posts.

WEEK 11 | READING: CHAPTERS 16 & 17

 WEEK 11 | FOCUS VIDEO

Watch the "Coaching Models" video.
- The Results Cycle
- Triple Loop Learning
- Coaching Funnel
- Johari Window
- GROW Model

 WEEK 11 | PROJECT: GROW MODEL

Practice the GROW model on a friend, or use it with a personal focus. Be prepared to discuss in peer meeting.

Practice the Coaching funnel on a friend, if time permits.

Be prepared to share your findings.

 WEEK 11 | PEER PREP

Consider your peer(s) and be prepared with a statement of affirmation to read about them during the last class. It should be only about a paragraph long and include your choice of the coaching value you feel is the strongest in their life (see the list starting on page 73 in the text).

WEEK 11 | PEER MEETING

Review Week 11
- Which of the coaching models works for you the most and why?
- Do you lean more easily toward giving Encouragement or Accountability? And how can you maintain a balance?
- On a scale of 1-10 how confident do you feel about your boundary setting? What would it take to move the number up (or maintain it well)?

COACHING PRACTICUM

This week will be your final observed coaching session. Talk with your client about progress made and what they want to do moving forward.

The need for support lies simply in the fact that if we could do it on our own we would have done it already.

Support = Encouragement and Challenge. If we have only one or the other we have problems.

Excess and Neglect Charts

SUPPORT

Enabling

Judging

Covering

Responsibility

Encouragement

Challenge

Encouragement is gracious. It sounds like, "I'm so proud of you" or even "That must be difficult."

Challenge is more direct. It says, "What do you think is happening?", "What is your next step then?" "How are you going to adjust things in order to move forward?"

Either way encouragement or challenge is a response to an active plan of forward movement.

Support is the healthy mean. It fosters strong partnerships and intentional growth.

Consider an ongoing situation you are walking through with someone. Look at the support diagram and put an "x" where you spend most of your energy. Add an arrow toward where you should be swinging if you need to make an adjustment. Put at "O" where you should be headed. Do this with at least two situations in your life.

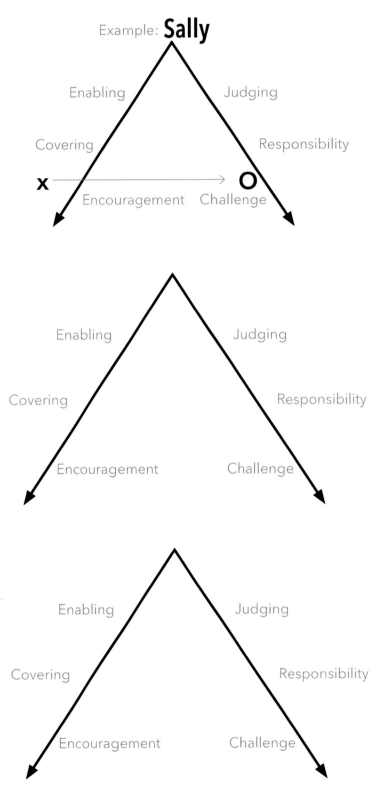

Write out your thoughts about the 2 situations you just graphed on the pendulum.

_____

_____

_____

_____

_____

_____

Consider a time when you were supported and it made all the difference. Write your thoughts here.

_____

_____

_____

_____

_____

_____

_____

Consider a time when you were challenged/fledged and you grew because of it. Write your thoughts here.

_____

_____

_____

_____

_____

_____

_____

BOUNDARIES

FROM COACH'S VIEW

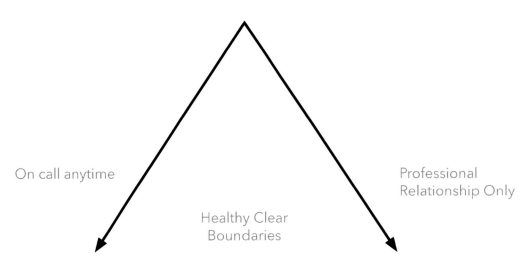

On call anytime

Professional
Relationship Only

Healthy Clear
Boundaries

> Do both parties know the clear answers to these questions:
>
> - Can a phone call be made at any time?
> - Is texting acceptable?
> - How would emergencies be handled?
>
> - What exactly is an emergency?
> - Are visits to my home welcome?
> - Are drop-in's okay at the office/house?

FROM COACHEE'S VIEW

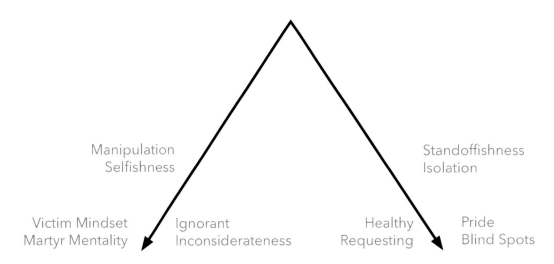

Manipulation
Selfishness

Standoffishness
Isolation

Victim Mindset
Martyr Mentality

Ignorant
Inconsiderateness

Healthy
Requesting

Pride
Blind Spots

How can we know who we are dealing with?
How can we maintain healthy helping relationships?
In coaching, the answer to most questions from the client is a question: *What is the Spirit of God telling you to do?*

What Time Is It?

Infantizing is a possibility that must be revisited. When we as coaches take an adult role in someone's life, we naturally label or sentence them to taking the role of a child.

Our job as coaches is to help people grow in their connection to God and His plans for their life. We are not intended to be a mediator who hears God for them. We can help by bouncing ideas around and support them by encouraging and challenging. Telling them what to do can be a dangerous place to take. (The exception is the immoral or unbiblical. We could not stand by and encourage that kind of 'practicing'.)

Boundaries are vitally important in helping another person grow to a healthy maturity for our own lives and families and others.

✏ Journal Time

Consider the pendulum of the coach's view. Any adjustments you need to make?

_____

_____

_____

_____

Consider the pendulum from the coachee's view. Anything you need to be more aware of with the people you are dealing with?

_____

_____

_____

⌛ One-Minute Takeaway
Take one minute to write down what stood out to you in this session.

_____

_____

_____

_____

_____

The Results Cycle

BELIEFS
what I hold to be true about people,
power, relationships, work, etc.

...which reinforce my...

...determine my...

RESULTS
the outcomes I create

BEHAVIOR
how I act and interact with others

...which affects the...

...which influences the...

QUALITY OF MY RELATIONSHIPS
the degree of openness, trust & support

From *The Heart of Coaching* by Thomas Crane

Triple Loop Learning

Single loop – affects behavior
Double loop – affects thinking
Triple loop – affects being

"Coaching people to create an Impossible Future always requires personal and organizational transformation. Transformation involves intervening in who people are (triple loop), which in turn influences their thinking (double) and behavior (single). The way you are being at any given time – an inspired leader or dull manage, excellent or mediocre, an activist or an analyst – determines what is possible and not passible. When a transformation occurs, something powerful happened in who people are being that is beyond a mere change in behavior. The person who is there now was not there before; the person who was there before does not exist."

from *Masterful Coaching* by Robert Hargrove

Coaching Funnel

Stuff
Issues
Dreams
Obstacles

GOAL/FOCUS

Exploration

OPTIONS

Evaluation
Outcomes

ACTION

New Focus?
New Options

Johari Window

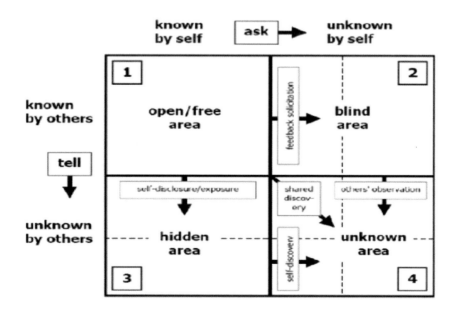

The Grow Model

- **Goal**
  What do you want?

- **Reality**
  Current situation?

- **Options**
  What could you do?

- **Will**
  What will you do?

Recycle to achieve your goal.

G - GOAL
Work through the Recognize/Focus parts of the ROAD

Set the hook by:
- Helping paint a picture of what life would look like if "arrived".
  - What is going to be different in your life when this is resolved?
  - What things are you not going to have to deal with if this is resolved?
  - What are the benefits of acquiring this?
- Asking questions that help them "sense" the win.
  - What will it feel like be "there"?
  - How will your life change when you arrive?
  - Why will this be worth it?

R - REALITY
This kind of corresponds with the O in ROAD for ownership. Basically it is a reality check and rills into what is actually happening now.

Reality focuses more on where the base line is. Questions could include:
- Where is the starting place?
- What is currently going on?
- What is the base line?

O - OPTIONS / OBSTACLES / OUTCOMES-
Some use Obstacles and Options, some just use Options, but the focus here must include some sort of working through of possibilities.

You can start with Obstacles if they were not addressed in the R-Reality phase.

This phase requires a lot of "If…. Then…." Kind of reasoning.

So the question progression would go something like this:

- What has been keeping you from moving ahead or addressing this?
- What are your options to move forward? Followed by- If you do that what will happen?

And then repeating all of the above as many times as needed till you get clarity on what the best possible next step could be.

At that point, with a chosen next step we move on to the W.

W - WILL (OR SOME SAY "WHAT'S NEXT?")
This is the point of engagement.

- What will you do then?
- How likely are you for that to actually happen? (there may be times when you have to revisit the "O" questions here)
- On a scale of 1 to 10—with 10 be absolutely sure I will move forward with this step— where would you place yourself?
- What would it take to move that number up a couple of notches?

BRIDGES COACHING

Coaching Session   Date: _____

Focus:_____

_____

_____

Coaching Appointment Notes:_____

_____

_____

_____

_____

_____

_____

_____

Action Steps for Next Coaching Appointment:

☐ _____

☐ _____

☐ _____

☐ _____

☐ _____

Concerns or Challenges:_____

_____

_____

_____

_____

_____

_____

NEXT APPOINTMENT   Date: _____   Time: _____

Coach Form

BRIDGES COACHING

Client Name: _____   Date: _____

Client Progress Report: _____

_____

_____

_____

_____

_____

_____

_____

Focus: _____

_____

_____

Coaching Appointment Notes: _____

_____

_____

_____

_____

_____

_____

Action Steps for Next Coaching Appointment:_____

_____

_____

_____

_____

_____

NEXT APPOINTMENT   Date: _____   Time: _____

BRIDGES COACHING

COACHING EVALUATION

Assess the coaching session you observed.

Coaching Asssessment

What percentage of the time was the coachee talking? _____

What was the goal of the client? _____
_____
_____

What was the most powerful question? _____
_____

What would you say was the strong suit in this session? _____
_____
_____

What action step(s) were agreed upon?
_____
_____
_____
_____
_____
_____
_____

Any questions you have:
_____
_____
_____
_____
_____

BRIDGES COACHING

Coaching Session   Date: _____

Focus:_____

_____

_____

Coaching Appointment Notes: _____

_____

_____

_____

_____

_____

_____

_____

_____

Action Steps for Next Coaching Appointment:

☐ _____

☐ _____

☐ _____

☐ _____

☐ _____

Concerns or Challenges:_____

_____

_____

_____

_____

_____

_____

NEXT APPOINTMENT   Date: _____   Time: _____

Coach Form

BRIDGES COACHING

Client Name: _____   Date: _____

Client Progress Report: _____

_____

_____

_____

_____

_____

_____

_____

Focus: _____

_____

_____

Coaching Appointment Notes: _____

_____

_____

_____

_____

_____

_____

Action Steps for Next Coaching Appointment: _____

_____

_____

_____

_____

_____

NEXT APPOINTMENT   Date: _____   Time: _____

BRIDGES COACHING

COACHING EVALUATION

Assess the coaching session you observed.

Coaching Asssessment

What percentage of the time was the coachee talking? _____

What was the goal of the client? _____
_____
_____

What was the most powerful question? _____
_____

What would you say was the strong suit in this session? _____
_____
_____

What action step(s) were agreed upon?
_____
_____
_____
_____
_____
_____
_____

Any questions you have:
_____
_____
_____
_____
_____

- Focus Video (optional)
- Journal Time (optional)
- Reading
- Project
- Second Project
- Peer Meeting
- Celebration Class

Additional Resource:
Ideas & Excerpts from
Masterful Coaching by Lynn
Grodzki and Wendy Allen

WEEK 12 | FOCUS VIDEO

Watch the "Types of Coaching" video (optional).

WEEK 12 | JOURNAL TIME: NICHE

Take some time and journal your initial thoughts regarding your personal coaching applications at this time.

WEEK 12 | READING: PART III & APPENDIX A

WEEK 12 | PROJECT: PICK 5

From Appendix A, pick 5 coaching principles that will come easily to you and 5 you will have to work on. Write the numbers in the blanks below. Bring to the final class to share with your peer partner.

Principles that will come easily to me...   Principles I will need to work on...

1) _____   1) _____

2) _____   2) _____

3) _____   3) _____

4) _____   4) _____

5) _____   5) _____

WEEK 12 | PROJECT: WRITTEN OUTCOMES

Consider the following terms. Write out a one sentence definition of each. You'll be amazed at what you have learned!

ACTIVE LISTENING_____

_____

ASKING POWERFUL QUESTIONS_____

_____

TRANSFORMATION_____

_____

SUCCESS_____

_____

RECOGNITION/ FOCUS_____

_____

OWNERSHIP_____

_____

ACTION STEPS_____

_____

DEDICATION_____

_____

JOURNEYING FROM HERE TO THERE _____

_____

TELLING_____

_____

Prep for Declaration of Use

Write out a one-sentence statement of use. Include where and how you intend to use what you have learned and be prepared to share with the class in the Course Celebration.

Examples:
- I plan to use casual coaching ongoing or as needed with my family, and my co-workers.
- I want to work with young women on destiny discovery.
- I will develop skills coaching and work with spiritual development.
- I want to help others through relationship coaching, specifically older couples.

_____

_____

 ## WEEK 12 | PROJECT: COACHING CULTURE COURSE EVALUATION

Please fill out the course evaluation survey online prior to the final class.

 ## WEEK 12 | PEER MEETING

Review week 12
- Share which coaching application intrigues you
- Talk about any niche ideas

Review course
- Review needed items for Coaching Celebration
- Bring up any questions about the coaching paradigm
- Talk about next steps

 ## WEEK 12 | COACHING CELEBRATION

Be prepared to finish one of these three sentences:
- "I'm so glad I took Bridges Coach Training because...."
- "My biggest take away from Bridges Coach Training will be..."
- "If you take Bridges Coach Training it will..."

Share Definitions from Written Outcomes
Pick 5
Possible Next Steps
Coaching Value Takeaways for Peer (p 73-77)
Declarations of Use
Certificate Presentations

TYPES OF COACHING

There are many different kinds of coaching and even personal niches that should be explored.

- Executive and Leadership Coaching
  - Two well-paid coaching specialties that add value and meaning to the work and lives of executives
- Business Coaching
  - Helping small-business owners and professionals in business learn to thrive.
- Skills Coaching
  - Skill based and peak performance coaching that gives clients far-reaching proficiency.
- Career Coaching
  - Showing clients how to design and implement an ideal career path, an essential resource for those in and out of the labor market. OR
  - Assisting clients in the recognition of their personal design and makeup thereby helping them choose appropriate next steps on their personal career pathway
- Life Coaching
  - The coaching specialty that helps motivated clients take steps to greatly improve their lives.
- Wellness Coaching
  - A new facet of holistic care, coaching people to take greater responsibility for their own health and well-being.
- Creativity Coaching
  - A coaching specialty that focuses on the expression and release of internal imagination and personal design
- Relationship Coaching
  - Helping clients navigate their personal relationships ranging from friendships to family members including these relationships:
    - Dating
    - Engagement
    - Marital
    - Parental
    - Friendship
    - Employer/Employee
    - Co-workers
    - Neighbors
    - Spiritual Coaching
- Spiritual Coaching
  - Coming alongside clients for accelerated Spiritual connection and growth
  - Helping clients find a place in the kingdom that suits who they were designed to be
- Special Interest Coaching
  - Working within a specific sphere of expertise or focus arena
- Casual Coaching
  - Using coaching in everyday conversation with family and friends
  - Using coaching intentionally as a ministry
- Self Coaching
  - Applying coaching principles to personal areas of intentional growth OR
  - Using coaching practices to apply to a specific area of concern or conflict
- As needed/ongoing coaching

Niche Areas or People Groups

A niche area defined is a certain area of interest and expertise that and individual identifies as a specific arena of intentional impact. These could focus on a particular issue from the past or a special interest.

Niche areas fall into two basic categories -could include:
- A specific skill
  - Writers
  - Speakers
  - Small Group leaders
  - Efficiency/Organization
  - Promotion
  - Sports
  - Parenting
- A specific issue
  - Abuse
  - Eating Disorder
  - Grief
  - Addiction

People groups are a similar category in that they typically narrow the focus to a certain group. This does not mean that the coach is not able to assist others out of this focused area, but that they are most comfortable with this particular group.

People groups could be divided by:
- Age
- Gender
- Location
- Association
- Passion
- Issue

 ## Journal Time

Which of the Niche areas could you see yourself in?
Is God prompting you toward something new?
Which people groups are you naturally drawn toward?

_____

_____

_____

_____

_____

_____

BRIDGES COACHING

Coaching Session   Date: _____

Focus:_____

_____

_____

Coaching Appointment Notes:_____

_____

_____

_____

_____

_____

_____

_____

Action Steps for Next Coaching Appointment:

☐ _____

☐ _____

☐ _____

☐ _____

☐ _____

Concerns or Challenges:_____

_____

_____

_____

_____

_____

_____

NEXT APPOINTMENT   Date: _____   Time: _____

BRIDGES COACHING

Coach Form

Client Name: _____   Date: _____

Client Progress Report: _____

_____

_____

_____

_____

_____

_____

_____

Focus: _____

_____

_____

Coaching Appointment Notes: _____

_____

_____

_____

_____

_____

_____

Action Steps for Next Coaching Appointment:_____

_____

_____

_____

_____

_____

NEXT APPOINTMENT   Date: _____   Time: _____

Coaching Questions

BRIDGES COACHING

BRIDGES COACHING OFFERS:

Personal Life Coaching
Video Online Coach Training
Life Coaching Certification
Professional Coaching Certifications
Destiny by Design Personal Pathway
Seminars, Group or Personal Workshops

Additional offerings of Bridges Coaching can be found at
WWW.BRIDGESCOACHING.NET
or contact Cindy Scott at cindy@bridgescoaching.net.

Made in the USA
Middletown, DE
31 January 2021